What's it like to be a...
PUPPETEER

Written by Susan Cornell Poskanzer
Illustrated by Diane Paterson

Troll Associates

Special Consultant: Peter Baird, *Director of Bil Baird's Marionettes, New York, New York.*

Library of Congress Cataloging-in-Publication Data

Poskanzer, Susan Cornell.
   Puppeteer / by Susan Cornell Poskanzer; illustrated by Diane
Paterson.
     p.   cm.—(What's it like to be a...)
   Summary: Before giving a performance, puppeteers, Max and Jane,
describe how they make and operate their puppets.
   ISBN 0-8167-1432-0 (lib. bdg.)   ISBN 0-8167-1433-9 (pbk.)
   1. Puppeteers—Juvenile literature. 2. Puppets and puppet-plays—
Juvenile literature. [1. Puppeteers. 2. Puppets.
3. Occupations.] I. Paterson, Diane, 1946-   ill. II. Title.
III. Series.
PN1972.P64 1989
791.5'3—dc19   88-10042

What's it like to be a...
PUPPETEER

Jane and Max look out on the grassy hill in the park. Now it is empty. But soon it will be covered with people. The people will laugh. They will shout. They will have a wonderful time with a proud dragon, a funny princess, and two dancing stars.

Jane and Max are the "Popcorn Puppeteers."
Each Saturday during the summer, they put on a
puppet show in the park.

"Good morning," says Jane to Ralph, the
dragon. The sock puppet has red and green scales
on its back. Jane slides Ralph onto her hand and
makes Ralph's mouth open and close. Then she
speaks for him in a soft, low voice.

"I was beginning to think you forgot about me," says Ralph.

Jane checks all the puppets to make sure they are ready for today's show.

Max sets up the puppet stage. He and Jane built the stage and made all of their puppets by hand. Max chooses the puppets for today's show and hangs them on hooks behind the stage. He puts Jane's puppets on one side. He puts his own puppets on the other side.

The stage has a see-through curtain, called a scrim. Jane and Max stand behind the scrim, while their puppets perform in front of it. Through the scrim, the puppeteers can see their puppets moving. They can also see their audience, without the audience seeing them.

Scrim

Max looks through the scrim now.

"Jamie and his grandmother are coming!"
says Max.

Jamie comes to every show given by the
Popcorn Puppeteers. He wants to be a puppeteer
when he grows up.

Every night, Jamie makes up puppet plays by making shadows in his room. He holds his hands up to the lamplight and casts shadows on the walls. Jamie started by making simple birds. Now he can shape all sorts of characters with his hands. He practices moving them. He gives a special voice to each one. Max showed Jamie how to make the shadows come alive.

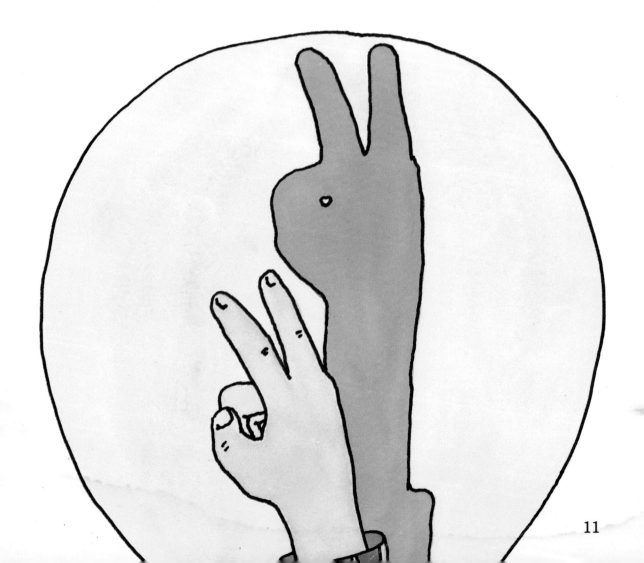

Jamie's grandmother loves puppets, too. She usually comes to the shows with Jamie. Today Jamie and his grandmother carry bright red balloons.

"Hi!" says Jamie.

"Will Ralph be in the show today?" Grandma asks Jane. "He's my all-time favorite puppet."

"You're in luck," beams Jane. "Today Ralph is in a new play we wrote. Would you like to watch while we rehearse?"

"You bet," Jamie says excitedly.

Jane takes out a mirror. (At home she uses her bathroom mirror.)

"This is how Ralph rehearses," she explains. "First, I look into the mirror. I move my face to see how I want Ralph to smile.

"Then Ralph tries out the smile. I also imagine how Ralph should look when he's angry, afraid, or surprised. Then we practice in the mirror. It takes months of practice, before Ralph and I can make just the faces we want."

Jamie and his grandmother laugh at Ralph's funny faces.

"Here's his surprised face," says Jane. "First, I throw his head back and tilt it to one side. Then I straighten him up and open his mouth wide. We have to study each part of looking surprised."

Jamie makes a surprised expression in the mirror.

"I had to think about Ralph's voice, too.
Ralph is a calm, proud dragon. So I gave him a
low, soft voice. After he had a voice, I practiced
with the mirror again to make his mouth move
along with the words."

"I like your voice," Jamie says to Ralph.

"The princess is a jumpy person who worries a lot," says Max. "That's why I gave her a high, bouncy voice."

"I'd like to stay and chat," says the princess, "but I must vacuum the palace. I'm busy, busy, busy!" The princess dashes about.

"The princess is a hand and rod puppet," explains Max. "My right hand fits inside her mouth to make it move. My left hand controls rods that make her hands move.

Some Sesame Street puppets are hand and rod puppets.

"Sock puppets like Ralph are great. But
Ralph must carry everything in his mouth. We
wanted to make the princess seem more like a
real person."

"How did you design the princess?" asks
Grandma. She touches the puppet's curly red
hair.

"I had an idea about a funny little red-haired princess," answers Max. "Whenever we have an idea for a puppet, we draw a picture of it, so we don't forget it. We keep all the pictures in a notebook."

Walking Salami puppet

Clown

Max shows Jamie his notebook. Jamie flips through pages and pages of wonderful drawings.

"I like the walking salami puppet best," says Grandma. They all laugh.

By now, there are many people sitting on the grassy hill.

"It's almost show time," says Jane. "Time to do finger exercises. We keep our finger and hand muscles strong, so we can move the puppets easily."

"Maybe someday I'll be a Popcorn Puppeteer, too," says Jamie.

Jane looks at Max. Max looks at Jane. Then
they both look at Jamie and Grandma.
   "Would you two like to be in today's show?"
asks Jane.

Jamie and his grandmother can hardly believe it!

Jane starts the music. The curtain opens. The audience sees a dark night. Two stars dance across the sky.

Backstage, Jamie and Grandma each move a metal rod. At the top of each rod is a star puppet. Back and forth! Up and down! The puppeteers make the stars dance in the night sky!

Soon Ralph and the princess dance out together. "I'm Ralph," says the dragon to the audience.

"I'm the princess," says the princess in her little, high voice.

The audience laughs as the princess bumps into Ralph.

"You're very clumsy," says Ralph to the princess. "My poor dragon toes! Won't you please try to dance like a princess?"

"I can't!" cries the princess. "A witch put a magic spell on my feet!"

The crowd loves the play. They laugh at the clumsy princess. They cheer when the magic spell is broken. They clap loudly at the end.

Now it is time for the puppeteers to take a bow. They skip out with the puppets still in their hands. Everyone applauds.

As Jamie bows, he looks out at the smiling faces on the hill. He is proud to be a real puppeteer.